STEAM MEMORIES 195___ ___s.

No.6: Great Eastern Lines:
Stratford, March, Cambridge, Ipswich & Branch Lines.

Book Law Publications

Copyright Book Law Publications 2007
ISBN 978-1901-945-836

INTRODUCTION

When photographer Don Beecroft visited the lines which made up the territory of the former Great Eastern Railway, he made a point of recording not only the scenes at the main centres but also those still to be found on the fast disappearing branch lines out in the country. This album contains images from all corners of the East Anglian lines although it by no means purports to be exhaustive in its coverage. What it does show is a representation of British Railways motive power and operations in that part of eastern England which, to many of us, was something of a 'backwater' with a lot of charm. BR themselves viewed most of the ex GER lines as something which they could best do without and withdrew many of the passenger and goods services long before steam itself was banished from the area.

Hopefully the illustrations herein show something of what became of the old GER in the latter days of the steam railway. We start 'in the country' looking at the various engine sheds and the residents therein. Next we go to Stratford for a quick tour of the vast complex, which was always came up with some surprise or other to visiting enthusiasts. Then on to Liverpool Street station before a quick visit to the LT&SR line, which became part of the Eastern Region early on after Nationalisation, although as a kind of 'poor relation', especially in latter years. Country stations are next on the itinerary before ending our tour at March engine shed - the northern outpost of the GE, so to speak. We have endeavoured to look north, south, east and west within our boundary and, hopefully, have come up with a balanced, pleasing and well illustrated album portraying the former lines of the GER in BR days.

(Front cover) B17 No.61657 DONCASTER ROVERS resides at March shed, the 'Footballer's' home depot in June 1956. BLP - DB122.

(title page) One-time pride of the GE Line locomotive fleet - the BR Standard 'Britannia' Pacific. This is No.70035 RUDYARD KIPLING at Stratford shed in March 1960. BLP - DB2950.

(rear cover) 'Britannia' No.70036 BOADICEA crosses onto the platform road at Cambridge with a Down London express in June 1959. BLP - DB1974.

Printed and bound by The Amadeus Press, Cleckheaton, West Yorkshire.
First published in the United Kingdom by Book Law Publications, 382 Carlton Hill, Nottingham, NG4 1JA.

There had been an engine shed at Hertford East since 1843 when the Northern & Eastern Railway opened a one-road building in October of that year. About 1858 another shed, this time a two-road affair sited east of the station, was erected by the GER. In 1966 the N&ER depot closed and in 1891 the GER shed was enlarged and new facilities were provided. In 1901 disaster struck when the roof was engulfed by fire, a common occurrence with such establishments. With a new roof in place the shed carried on its function until about 1955 when yet another new roof was provided by BR. At the same time the walls were strengthened and one of the two roads was extended through the rear wall. Finally, to round off its history, the shed was closed on 21st November 1960 ending over one hundred years of locomotive facilities at this place. Throughout much of that time Hertford East was a sub to Stratford and in July 1957 one of the resident engines was J15 No.65463 looking typically scruffy and unkempt like most of the Stratford fleet at that time. The 0-6-0 did not outlive the shed and was condemned in November 1959, aged 47 years - young by J15 standards. *BLP - DB423.*

F5 No.67203 spent all of its fifty-two year life allocated to Stratford shed since new in June 1905. In June 1956, as one of five such F5's fitted with vacuum controlled push-pull gear and allocated to work the Epping-Ongar shuttle service, it was out-stationed at Epping, one of Stratford's numerous small sub sheds (above). The five engines were fitted with the P&P gear in September 1949 and were numbered 67193, 67200, 67202, 67203 and 67213 - all of them lost their Westinghouse equipment at the same time but were also fitted with trip-cock gear. The latter was then a requirement for locomotives working over or onto lines operated by London Transport. The necessity for P&P working over this short section of the Loughton line came about when London Transport extended the Central Line electric service from Loughton to Epping on 25th September 1949 leaving the six-mile long, single track, Epping-Ongar section to be worked by British Railways steam locomotives. The line in question was single between the two places but at the intermediate station of North Weald a crossing place, with electrical interlocking, was used. At the inauguration of the new service, Ongar had a train leaving for Epping every 20 minutes during the morning and evening rush hours whilst a 40 minute services sufficed outside those periods. On Sundays some through services continued beyond Stratford to Liverpool Street bringing the rare sight on P&P trains into the terminus - two catch the two return services you had to be something of an early bird. As for the engine shed at Epping, LT financed the rebuilding of the two road building from its original 1893 style with a northlight pattern roof, to this brick and concrete affair. Coaling was carried out from open wagons and the 50ft turntable already in situ was retained for the goods tender engines. *BLP - DB108.*

4

J15 No.65440 was one of three of its class to be fitted with trip cocks for working the suburban goods services over the Loughton-Ongar line from early 1948. The other two J15's were Nos.65450 and 65455. Epping engine shed was home to this particular engine in July 1957, during the last months of the steam P&P operation. High drama visited the branch on 7th June 1957 when the push-pull set being propelled by F5 No.67193 was partially derailed when a Hawker Hunter jet fighter crashed near the line. Other more welcome visitors, though complete strangers, arrived during August 1956 when there was a shortage of F5's. First along was a King's Cross based N2 No.69546 which came on the 9th and was joined on the 14th by Neasden BR Standard Cl.4 No.76041. Both engines were trip cock fitted but had to run round their trains at both Epping and Ongar. Apparently points which had not been used for some time were employed. The strangers left at some time during the third week of August. During 1955 a Neasden N5 No.69257 was loaned to Epping for a number of months because one of the regular engines, F5 No.67213 had been cut up at Stratford by mistake! Going further back in time, 'fitted' C12 No.67363 was sent from Annesley to Epping on the last day of May 1953 to help out with a shortfall of F5's. The former GN Atlantic tank was not fitted with trip cock gear but it managed to work the services to Ongar until mid August when it returned to Nottinghamshire. London Transport extended their underground services to Ongar on Monday 18th November 1957, the BR service having been suspended after the last trains on Saturday 16th. For the last day of steam services F5's Nos.67200, 67212 and 67218 were in attendance. The latter engine was not one of those initially fitted with P&P gear for the Ongar route but was fitted at the same time for the Yarmouth-Beccles line along with 67199. The shed at Epping closed with the departure of the steam locomotives. As for the locomotives themselves - all the tank engines succumbed shortly afterwards, their specialist equipment being surplus to requirements but the 0-6-0 tender engines lasted slightly longer and made a brief return to the line in 1959. *BLP - DB443.*

5

There had been an engine shed at Sudbury since July 1849. Built by the rather long-windedly named Colchester, Stour Valley, Sudbury & Halstead Railway, the shed stood in the north-west corner of the large goods yard which was the terminus of the then branch from Marks Tey. By 1950 the shed was apparently in dire straits and required extensive rebuilding (renewal more like) but that did not happen and demolition became the only option but that did not occur until July 1956 when the place became a dangerous derelict hovel requiring timber shoring on each corner. A stabling/servicing point was then created for the usual two locomotives outstationed there from Cambridge and Bury St Edmunds for the passenger and goods services. This is E4 No.62785, in July 1957, at the long abandoned terminal platform of the erstwhile first passenger station at Sudbury. The passenger facilities here had apparently ceased in 1865 when a new station was opened on the through route between Long Melford and Chapel & Wakes Colne. Sudbury 'shed' was sub to Bury St Edmunds but Cambridge usually supplied the 'residents' which on most occasions were J15 0-6-0s for both passenger and goods working, and Sudbury yard pilot - Sudbury men of course manned the engines up to closure in October 1959. *BLP - DB426.*

Cambridge J15 No.65442, in a rather woebegone condition, completes the duo of outstationed locomotives at Sudbury on this July Saturday in 1957. This part of the town was full of railway connections, the lane at the top of the goods yard was named Great Eastern Road. There was a public house called the Great Eastern Hotel although this could at one time have been a railway hotel belonging to the GER ? In 1927 the town had a population of nearly six and half thousand souls. It was, according to the Railway & Commercial Gazetteer, fifty-eight miles from London and was served by one station. Besides agricultural connections, breweries could be counted amongst its industry. In 1938, the Railway Clearing House Official Handbook of Stations claimed it could boast no less than eight private sidings besides full goods station accommodation including a one and a half ton crane. Certain aspects of these photographs reveal an apparently still busy goods facility in 1957. Happily Sudbury station is still operational, though the goods yard no longer exists. Once again the place is a terminus, at the end of the single line branch from Marks Tey. *BLP - DB429.*

The locomotive facility was abandoned here in early 1959 by which time a single steam locomotive, usually a J15, again supplied by Cambridge shed, shared the Bury St Edmunds to Sudbury via Long Melford passenger service with a diesel railbus of German origin. This final view in July 1957 shows the E4 and J15 simmering away in this not so quiet backwater. It was reported that on 6th August 1957 two B12's, Nos.61549 (of Cambridge) and 61570 (of Ipswich) were working local trains on the Sudbury branch - sledge hammers and nuts come to mind. The line through Sudbury was often used as a diversionary route for holiday trains and on 20th July 1957 a Manchester-Clacton, Saturdays Only through express passed with B17 No.61660 HULL CITY in charge. No.65442 was a veteran from 1899 and had spent the whole of its long life in the area at either Cambridge, Colchester or Bury St Edmunds sheds. It was condemned less than a year after this photograph caught it in the old terminus. The E4, also from the Cambridge allocation, was a little bit older than the 0-6-0 by four and a half years and it stayed operational for a while longer too being withdrawn in December 1959. It then passed into preservation as part of the National Collection. *BLP - DB432.*

Since delivery from the Sentinel factory in October 1930 as LNER No.63, this Y3 class 0-4-0 had been working within the boundary of the old Great Eastern Railway. Its first shed was Colchester and after ten years there it moved on to Lowestoft in October 1940, not a good time to be by the seaside at that place. Six months later it moved inland to Norwich but two weeks afterwards it was called to Cambridge. Whilst at the Chesterton Civil Engineer depot in Cambridge it was renumbered to 8163 in June 1946. Later it was allocated 68163 by British Railways but never carried that number because, in July 1948, it was transferred back to Lowestoft to work for the Civil Engineer in the large sleeper depot at that place. The Sentinel became part of the Service Stock fleet and at the end of April 1953 it was eventually renumbered to Departmental No.40 and is seen near its engine shed in the Sleeper Works at Lowestoft during August 1955. Note the necessary wire cage spark arrester over the chimney. Besides No.40, there was also No.38 a similar Y3 which arrived at Lowestoft from Stratford in January 1950. Then there was No.41 which had been around the place since January 1936. In July 1961 a latecomer arrived from Boston Hall Hills Sleeper Depot, Y3 No.7, formerly 68166. Another Y3, No.8178 (later Departmental 42) had worked this place until July 1952 when it moved to Cambridge. No.40 was condemned on 23rd May 1964 along with No.7. No.41 was condemned on 30th March 1963 whilst No.38 had succumb in February 1959 and was broken up on site which was probably the fate of Nos.7, 40 and 41. The engine which housed these Sentinel locomotives had two sets of rails but at different gauges, standard gauge and narrow gauge for the locomotives used within the Works internal railway system. The shed was apparently fairly modern structure having been erected by BR in the early 1950's to replace an earlier wooden shed built by the LNER during the 1920's. The BR shed closed in May 1964 when the remaining Sentinel's were condemned. *BLP - DB951.*

The former Midland & Great Northern Railway (Eastern & Midlands Railway) engine shed at Cromer Beach was under the control of Melton Constable until 20th September 1954 but after that date the small one-road depot became a sub-shed of Norwich Thorpe. The change came about because the former Great Eastern line to Cromer High (East Norfolk Railway) had been closed and all services diverted to Cromer Beach station. Likewise the engine shed at Cromer High was closed, its engines and duties being transferred to Cromer Beach engine shed. A week after its new found importance, on Sunday 26th September 1954, Cromer Beach shed had the following engines stabled: B1 No.61048, B12 No.61540, B17 Nos.61656, 61665, 61666, and motor fitted N7 No.69690 which worked the Mundesley-on-Sea branch. It must have been quite cramped. In July 1957 the shed had a lot less visitors and B12 No.61542 of Norwich Thorpe (above) was resting alongside the single road building. The original 47ft turntable which was situated just west of the shed, near the coaling stage, and carried the only track leading to the shed, was taken out and a new larger table was laid down into the available space to the rear of the shed and, to enable B12 class 4-6-0s to use the facilities. (opposite) On the same day that No.61542 was resident, Stratford B12 No.61519 was making its way out of the shed, in dramatic fashion, to take up a passenger working. Because it was a sub shed with no fixed allocation, Cromer Beach had a varied and interesting number of visitors and short term residents. Residing at the shed on Sunday 31st March 1957 were B1's Nos.61046 and 61048 (both Norwich), with B12's Nos.61547 (Norwich) and 61570 (Ipswich). It was reported that five B12's were allocated to Cromer Beach depot in 1958 but this was not a permanent transfer and was merely an instruction that five of the class would be available for workings from the place during the summer months. By then of course the B12 class was becoming pretty deleted and finding five serviceable engines at any one time must have been quite taxing for those concerned. It was not unusual having 'Britannia's visiting the shed during the summer season on trains from Norwich. *BLP - DB446 & 447*.

Another Midland & Great Northern engine shed under review in this album is Melton Constable. Once the heart of the M&GN empire, Melton provided all the locomotive repair and maintenance facilities in the locomotive works adjacent to the engine shed. When the LNER took over the operations of the railway in 1938, the native motive power was anything but healthy and only a small proportion of the available motive power was retained, the rest being broken up at Stratford over the next couple of years. The LNER was forced to draft in numerous locomotives and various classes were used on the line, especially during the war years when the strategic value of certain sections of the M&GN became apparent. British Railways carried on where the LNER left off and one of the most successful classes to be employed on the line was the Ivatt LMS Class 4 tender engine of which it was claimed - by the men from Melton - could do anything asked of it and was a superb addition to the line. Melton Constable and the other former M&GN engine sheds had more than thirty-four of these excellent 2-6-0s between them. No.43147, note the Eastern Region route availability code on the cab - R.A.4, was one of the M&GN Section engines and was fitted accordingly with a tablet catcher for single line working. It is being got ready on Melton shed for another foray into the country whilst J67/2 No.68536 is likewise made ready for a day's work in July 1957. The engine shed here was a three road affair, rebuilt in 1951 from a similar brick and timber building erected by the Lynn & Fakenham Railway during 1881 ready for its 9th January 1882 opening. Closure came in March 1959 when the whole of the mainly single line M&GN system was closed for good. Like most of the Ivatt moguls used on the M&GN, No.43147 arrived at Melton when new. On closure it was transferred to Boston on the opposite side of the Wash. *BLP - DB461.*

Staying up near the Wash but going back in time slightly to July 1951 we meet C12 No.67356 at King's Lynn engine shed shortly after its arrival from South Lynn, where it had spent the previous fortnight after transfer from King's Cross. The 4-4-2t was not looking its best and appears to have been rubbing itself against a similar hard object with resultant damage. Note the push & pull gear which had been fitted to five of the class between January 1948 and October 1949. No.67356 was sent to King's Cross to join No.67374 working the Finsbury Park-Alexandra Palace service in May 1949. Meanwhile No.67386 was sent to King's Lynn to work the shuttle service to and from South Lynn M&GN station. Both the 'Top Shed' engines eventually joined 67386 at King's Lynn with 67374 settling in nicely for a seven year residency alongside 67386. Our C12 was not so lucky. Shortly after this picture was taken in that summer of 1951, the Atlantic tank was called to Doncaster and after entering the works on Thursday 6th September it was promptly condemned and then cut up. *BLP - DB5172.*

During the BR period the allocation of Cambridge engine shed was not much different from what it had been some twenty years previously in the pre-war era of the LNER. Admitted, by 1956 the Great Northern Atlantics, which were so popular on the fast trains to King's Cross, had all gone for scrap but their place had been taken by other former LNER motive power such as the Gresley B17 and the Thompson B2 rebuilds of that class. This is B17/6 No.61621 HATFIELD HOUSE in the shed yard at Cambridge in June 1956, one year and five months after it had been rebuilt to a Part 6 engine with a Diagram 100A boiler, as used by the Thompson B1. No.61621 required another 'General' in October 1956 - they were rather expensive to keep operational these B17's. Just two years after that, in November 1958, yet another heavy overhaul was required but by then 'the writing was on the wall' for this class and so Doncaster Works condemned and scrapped the twenty-eight year engine. *BLP - DB112.*

Being a former Great Eastern engine shed, Cambridge still had a large allocation of Stratford products on its books in June 1959 and amongst them was J69/1 No.68609. One of the 120 passenger tank versions of its class, the 0-6-0T was, as can be seen, in store at this time and would remain so until November when it was transferred to Stratford - no longer required by Cambridge. Except for three months during the winter of 1952-53, when it was at Bury St Edmunds shed, this engine had spent all of its life at Cambridge. All through that period from June 1901, Stratford Works had maintained and had fitted eleven different boilers. It carried the Westinghouse equipment until it was condemned in September 1962 and that brake was supplemented by a vacuum ejector fitted in April 1935. For these comfort of passengers in the trains it hauled, the 0-6-0T was fitted out with steam heating in May 1930 - one can only guess what passengers prior to that date had to put up with during previous winters. *BLP - DB1973.*

At an earlier date, August 1951 to be more precise, we meet C12 No.67360 at Cambridge engine shed shortly after it had returned from a General overhaul (its last) at Doncaster. This was another former Great Northern engine which had found employment in ex Great Eastern country by way of being transferred to the M&GN in March 1937. For that deployment the Atlantic tank had been fitted with a tablet exchanger for single line working but that was removed in July 1944. In the meantime No.4502, as it was then numbered, had been allocated to Yarmouth Beach shed, then in February 1940 it moved inland to Norwich and after three months there it went to Cambridge. Back to the M&GN in July 1940, at Melton Constable shed, it once again moved to Norwich for two weeks in December 1940. Then it returned to Cambridge for a twelve year stint during which time it became No.67360. Bury St Edmunds depot borrowed the 4-4-2T from October 1952 until July 1953 but its return to Cambridge was brief, leaving there for King's Lynn on 4th October 1953. It was condemned on 22nd January 1955 and cut up at Doncaster after nearly fifty-six years of service. *BLP - DB5173.*

This is the former Great Eastern engine shed at South Town in Yarmouth during August 1948, with resident D16/2 No.62553 dominating the picture. On the eve of Nationalisation this depot had fifteen of these 4-4-0 tender engines on its books, although some would be housed at the other exGER engine shed in Great Yarmouth at Vauxhall, on the other side of the Yare estuary. This aspect shows the rear, southern end, of the shed with its sheerlegs which allowed a wide scope of maintenance and repair to be carried out by the small detachment of fitters. For a seaside town bordering in size between small and medium, population 39,724 in 1927, Great Yarmouth was well served with three terminal stations and three engine sheds. None of the stations were grandiose affairs but their names reflected those of the engine sheds - Beach, South Town and Vauxhall. The former was of M&GN origin whilst the other two were ex Great Eastern Railway. In terms of size Beach, opened in 1903, was the largest with four roads and mechanical coaling facilities, with a reasonable allocation of between twenty and thirty engines depending on the season. Beach shed closed along with the bulk M&GN system in March 1959. Considering they were the last into town, the M&GN's passenger station enjoyed probably the best position in the resort in terms of walking distance to the beach and nearness to the various retail outlets and amusement amenities. The two GE stations on the other hand, were cut off from the commercial section of the town by tidal rivers, albeit narrow but nevertheless bridges were required for access. Vauxhall shed was another two road building but was longer than South Town. It dated from 1883 and was also closed in 1959 but predating the M&GN establishment by a couple of months. Also in this view are B17 No.61661 SHEFFIELD WEDNESDAY and F4 No.67154, both resident engines at this time. The B17 carries the green livery and associated lining applied in April 1948 during a 'Paint only' visit to Doncaster Works. *BLP - DB5169.* 17

It states in the notes that this picture depicts an aspect of Yarmouth South Town engine shed on an unknown day in July 1957. The engine is Norwich based J15 No.65472 under a coaling shelter. The other locomotives in view are unidentified but the nearest seems to be a D16. The location I am not so sure about but the J15 has just, it appears, undergone an overhaul with its paintwork reflecting some of the cleanliness associated with an engine having had a 'General' recently. No.65472 had indeed visited Stratford Works for such an event between 19th May and 24th June 1957 - its last overhaul incidentally. Moreover, it was transferred from Norwich Thorpe to Yarmouth South Town shed on 7th July 1957, although the smokebox door still wears the 32A shedplate rather than the 32D plate you would expect. However, it could be that the J15 has just arrived (only two weeks out of shops) and the fitters had yet to take off the plate and replace it with one of their own. Also, the engine was transferred back to Norwich nine weeks later, on 15th September, and therefore, perhaps, it was simply 'on loan' to South Town and the replating was not deemed necessary. *BLP - DB428.*

Shortly after being rebuilt from a Part 2 engine, D16/3 No.62613 was allocated to Yarmouth South Town engine shed on Tuesday 11th January 1949. This picture shows it in July 1957 just a month or so after completing its last General overhaul and still looking very smart. In 1930 the 4-4-0 had the dubious distinction of perhaps setting a record as to the number of transfers between the same two sheds in one twelve month period. On Saturday 22nd February 1930, fairly fresh out of shops, it transferred from Stratford, its home since new in June 1923, to Southend shed. On Saturday 15th March it was back at Stratford but transferred again to Southend on Saturday 29th of that month. Three weeks later, on Saturday 19th April it returned to Stratford but a month later on Saturday 17th May went back to Southend. On Saturday 14th June Stratford pulled it back in but let go a week later on Saturday 21st for its return to Southend. Things then settled down but on Saturday 8th November Stratford recalled the D16 and kept hold of it for fourteen years until Friday 18th November 1944 when Colchester was the recipient. Was it given a nickname by the Southend men? If so, what was it? Before Yarmouth South Town shed closed this engine moved on to the former Midland shed at Peterborough Spital Bridge on 12th April 1959. Its final move was to March depot on the last day of January 1960. It was condemned on 25th October 1960 and cut up at its birth place. *BLP - DB433.*

19

D16/3 No.62561 had been allocated to the former Midland & Great Northern engine shed at Yarmouth Beach in February 1949. In the July of that year we see the 4-4-0 on the shed yard, overlooked by some nice properties on Lesley Road. Note the tablet catcher on the tender near the cab doorway. This was fitted at the 4-4-0's last visit to Stratford Works (15th December 1948 to 1st February 1949) when **BRITISH RAILWAYS** was applied to the tender and the correct type of number 6 made up the BR renumbering. No.62562 was destined now to spend the rest of its life working the lines of the former M&GN system, its next transfer would take it to Norwich in September 1952 then, on 26th September 1955 it would venture further into the system and end its days at Melton Constable shed. It was condemned on 10th February 1958 and later cut up at Stratford. Note, in front of the D16, the rather immaculate tender with equally immaculate LNER lettering! Now which engine did that belong to? *BLP - DB5170.*

The engine shed at Bury St Edmunds comprised this wooden gabled building which had brick walls and a corrugated asbestos pitched roof with a central smoke vent running the whole length. Windowless walls made the inside of the shed extremely dark, dependant on artificial lighting. The original shed, built in 1904, had a northlight pattern roof but over the years up to Nationalisation the roof deteriorated so much that this non-standard affair was erected by the Eastern Region. The shed stood on the north side of the line west of the station and in June 1956 the allocation stood at about twenty locomotives. D16/3 No.62566 had been on the Bury allocation since 10th December 1939 after spending the whole of the 1930's swapping between Cambridge and King's Lynn sheds. It was at this time due for another 'General' and in October it would journey south to Stratford for that, its last overhaul, to take place. A transfer in June 1957 would see it leave Bury St Edmunds and return to King's Lynn to work out its last eighteen months prior to withdrawal. *BLP - DB121.*

Later on, during this June day in 1956, a couple more D16 Part 3 engines came on shed at Bury St Edmunds, King's Lynn based No.62601 and Cambridge based No.62553. Both these 4-4-0s were only six months away from condemnation and scrapping at Stratford on 1st January 1957. No.62601 had not been to Works since October 1954 and was due a new boiler but that was not to happen. Since coming into traffic in March 1911 this engine had carried no less than nineteen different boilers during its near forty-six year life. The Great Eastern area had a bad record of boiler damage due to indifferent water supplies which ranged from mediocre to bad. No.62553 was no different because it too last had a boiler change in October 1954 and was also due another one, it's lifetime tally of boilers since December 1906 was a more respectable seventeen. *BLP - DB117.*

The shed here at Bury closed on 5th January 1959, a victim of dieselisation and dropping passenger and goods traffic, although the drive to bring in the former was real reason for its early demise. Nevertheless, the shed was kept open for diesels until June 1959 when more of the Region's dedicated diesel depots started to take in the new motive power. When the end came for steam in this area it was both sudden and ruthless. In June 1956 it was still business as usual as far as steam traction was concerned, there was not much change happening except for the infiltration of a few diesel shunters of indifferent performance. D16/3 No.62618, one of the LNER built engines of this class - were they really pushing out engines in 1923 with fancy valances like that? - was another visitor to Bury having worked in from Cambridge. Considering its paintwork is verging on grimy, its metalwork is nicely polished which was probably down to its crew. This 4-4-0 had a somewhat longer future than the other three we have just seen. In March 1957 it went to Stratford for a 'General' and came out in early May. It transferred to King's Lynn in March 1958 but moved on to March shed during the following November. Withdrawn in November 1959, it was later cut up at Stratford. *BLP - DB109.*

23

Throughout the British Railways period Stratford Works carried out Heavy Intermediate repairs to the Eastern Region based Ivatt Class 4 2-6-0 tender engine allocation. Both the 'Old' and 'New' (High Meads) works at Stratford were involved in the maintenance of this class which usually had their 'General' repairs undertaken at Doncaster 'Plant' works. No.43160 of Yarmouth Beach shed, is seen alongside the 'Old' works in June 1958. The 'mogul' was one of five of its kind allocated new to Yarmouth in 1952, No.43160 was the penultimate member of the class and arrived at 32F in the August of that year along with Nos.43157, 43158, 43159 and 43160 - all Doncaster built. The 2-6-0 moved to Norwich Thorpe shed in February 1959 and then, in December 1960, to the former Great Central shed at Staveley. However, its residence at Staveley was rather short because less than a month later it went to Grimesthorpe shed in Sheffield until August 1961. Its final call was to Colwick where it rejoined many of its classmates until withdrawn in January 1965, less than thirteen years old. The corrugated asbestos clad building, forming the immediate background, was a fairly new 'shop' comprising a weigh bridge and store, built on the site of the erstwhile Northern & Eastern Railway polygonal roundhouse which existed as a wheel shop until just after WW2, locomotives having deserted the place in the 1880's. *BLP-DB773*.

During its time as a centre for locomotive repair, building and cutting up, not to mention the Carriage & Wagon departments, Stratford required a dedicated fleet of shunting engines some of which had to be capable of accessing all areas of the workshops and yards. Within the latter mentioned places of the 'Old' works, tracks with very tight curvature were a feature of the Polygon yard which required locomotives with very short wheelbases. Hence the employment, since January 1921, of this Class Y4 0-4-0T - Departmental No.33. With the locomotive shops of the 'Old' works forming the background in, June 1958, Departmental No.33 was the sole remaining member of Y4 class, its recruitment to Service Stock in September 1952 giving it an extension of life which took it to the closure of the 'Old' workshops in December 1963. Originally renumbered by BR to 68129 in October 1948, this engine spent all of its life within the confines of the Stratford complex, being helped in its duties by engines of other classes with similar wheelbases. The four other members of Y4 class, all allocated to Stratford running shed, had been employed mainly within the goods yards around East London at locations where, once again, sharp track curvature forbade the use of six-coupled engines. However, their employment was gradually taken away as either diesel shunters took on the work or the work disappeared altogether in the general loss of traffic being suffered by BR at that time. All four were cut up at Stratford between September 1955 and October 1957. Ironically No.33 was not broken up at Stratford but was instead sold for scrap to a merchant in Norwich. *BLP-DB774.*

Also at Stratford in June 1958, a filthy exGreat Eastern 0-6-0 No.65463 of Class J15 makes its way south past the former carriage shops. This engine had not had a 'General' nor any other type of overhaul since September 1955 and excepting for shed maintenance, would not be given any more. Stratford based from May 1947, the forty-six years old 0-6-0 had spent much of its life shedded 'out in the country' at places such as Colchester, Lowestoft, Norwich, and Yarmouth; this was its fourth spell at Stratford and was to prove to be its last prior to withdrawal in November 1959. Note that the tender of the Ivatt Cl.4, seen in a previous view, is adorned with the incorrect version of the new British Railways emblem. *BLP-DB775.*

One of the marvellous things about Stratford, in fact the former Great Eastern lines in general during BR days, was the large number of ancient locomotives still in existence. This is E4 No.62797 at Stratford in June 1958. Looking somewhat neglected and minus worksplate, the engine lies condemned and ready to be called into shops for cutting up. Some eighteen of these 2-4-0 tender engines managed to survive into BR days from a class total of one hundred at Grouping. No.62797's last shed, before withdrawal in the previous March, had been Cambridge and prior to that Lowestoft, nothing surprising about that but some of its LNER allocations were far more adventurous. In September 1935 No.7416, as it was then numbered, was given a thorough overhaul at Stratford. Coming out of the works on 10th October, it was then sent to North Eastern Area to begin a six year residence working over some of the most picturesque routes the area had to offer. Five other E4's joined it on the trek but they were split up amongst various sheds in the area. No.7416's first shed was Middleton-in-Teesdale where from 19th October 1935 to 30th July 1938 it plied the branch to Barnard Castle and on to Darlington, an idyllic life indeed. For the final months of 1938 it was allocated to Darlington shed from where it did virtually the same job but in reverse order. In December 1938 it moved over the Pennines for six months at Penrith, rubbing shoulders with the LMS contingent there. Finally it spent two years and five months at Kirkby Stephen before returning south to Norwich during the dark days of November 1941. So, this old-timer had had been around. Nearly fifty-six years old when condemned, it had given a good account of itself. Now there was only one of its kind left - No.62785 - and that went into preservation. *BLP - DB778.*

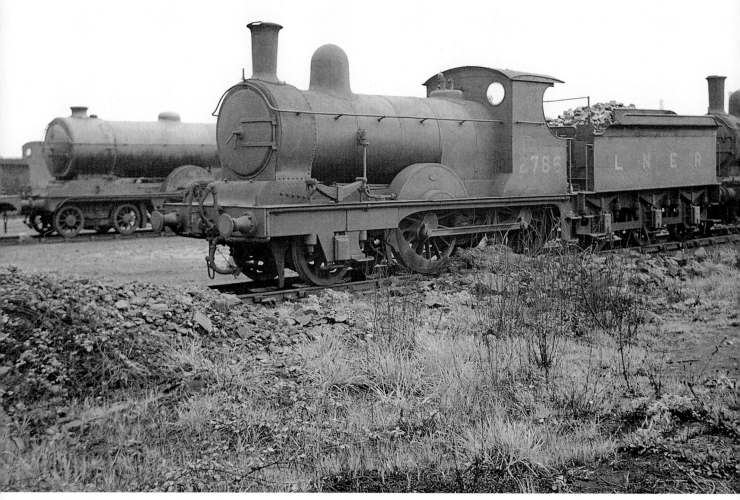

Going back to early April 1948, we find another E4 in virtually the same position at Stratford as No.62797. However, No.2786 was not condemned and was merely awaiting entry into works for a Light overhaul which would engage it from 7th April to 9th June - a long time indeed for such an insignificant repair but the procedure carried out to the paintwork of the E4 might explain away some of the two month delay. In this view the Cambridge based 2-4-0 was still sporting its four digit LNER number and had the former company initials adorning its tender sides but not for much longer because on release to traffic in June it would carry its full BR number on the cab sides whilst the tender would have BRITISH RAILWAYS painted in full 10 inch high Gill sans lettering. A smokebox numberplate was absent from that particular 'shopping' and would not be applied until a 'General' in June 1949. This engine was to enjoy another 'General' in late 1952 and because of that overhaul its life was extended to July 1956 making it sixty-one years old at withdrawal. The engine returned to Cambridge shed after its 1948 repair but moved across to Bury St Edmunds in July 1949 doing much the same as it had done since the mid-30's, plying along the rural byways of Cambridgeshire, Suffolk and Norfolk. In March 1952 Cambridge had the E4 back again to join the handful of other 2-4-0 tender engines in its care. *BLP - DB5162.*

Tucked away with what appears to be an unidentified J17 on a siding at the western end of the Stratford engine shed yard in June 1958, was this filthy (par for the course) resident J15 No.65361. This J15 had come to Stratford shed in February 1957 from Ipswich and was immediately sent into works for a much needed, six-week long, General overhaul. By now No.65361 was approaching its seventieth birthday and by some intervention by Stratford Works it was able to surpass that goal and reach seventy-four by the time of its condemnation in June 1962. Although spending much of its time on the GE lines at Cambridge shed, the J15 started wandering northwards in August 1938 and ended up at New England shed where it remained for four years. In a final flurry of wartime exploits it went further north on 17th October 1942 on transfer to Doncaster. One week later it reallocated to Mexborough from where it wintered through 1942 into 43. With the coming springtime No.7836, as it was then numbered, returned south to home territory and Stratford. However, on the way it called in at Melton Constable, or rather diverged somewhat onto the M&GN, from 19th April to 1st May, after which it proceeded to London, its wandering completed. The unidentified 0-6-0 keeping the 'old-timer' company appears to be one of those which at some time had tenders fitted with weather boards. In the left background of this picture we can see the High Meads erecting shop whilst to the right we have the lines of locomotives stabled on the tracks radiating from the 'Jubilee' shed. Note the diesel mechanical shunters starting to invade the premises. *BLP - DB779.*

29

Staying over on the west side of the Stratford complex, we are looking from the turntable across at the siding laid out in front of the timber sheds which backed onto the Channelsea river. These couple of sidings were used to stable engines which had just undergone repair at either of the two workshops or those engines awaiting entry. Ipswich B12 No.61566 had just completed a 'General' and on Sunday 2nd May 1948 is seen waiting its turn to go back into traffic. Since being built in May 1920, this 4-6-0 had been allocated to just three sheds Norwich, Yarmouth and the aforementioned Ipswich. It had been resident at this latter shed since October 1944 and would continue to be so until a final move to Norwich in June 1958, its sixth time at Thorpe. It would, however, do little work from 32A during those last six months of 1958 and was condemned on 26th January 1959. Note that it too had BRITISH RAILWAYS painted on the tender during this interim period prior to application of the BR crest. *BLP - DB5168.*

For another look at ex-works locomotives at the Channelsea end of Stratford, we go fairly modern at least in LNER locomotive terms, and meet Stratford based J39 No.64784 in June 1958 shortly after it had undergone its last 'General'. This was yet another wandering soul which ended up at Stratford. Starting life at Darlington Works in May 1929, the 0-6-0 was put into traffic at York shed but after just one day there it was transferred to Glasgow and started work from Eastfield depot. During the war it was allocated to St Margarets shed April 1943 and towards the end of the conflict ended up at Carlisle Canal in March 1945. In July 1946 it ventured north again and went to Thornton Junction shed. During the following November Dundee beckoned for a ten month spell. Finally, as far as the LNER were concerned, it was sent south to Norwich and got there on 21st September 1947. Stratford got the J39 in October 1951 and it remained at the east London depot until withdrawal in August 1960. Besides having a wanderlust regarding its sheds, the 0-6-0 had an interesting 'shopping' history. Its first works visits was to Cowlairs as soon as it arrived in Scotland in 1929. Thereafter it was 'shopped' at Cowlairs until the end of 1945, its last 'General' being carried out at the former NBR workshop in December 1945. The next works to host it was Stratford in November 1947 but in August/September 1948 it was up at Gorton for a 'General'. However, during the early 1950's the former LNER workshops on BR had a shortage of space for outstanding repairs and the former Midland and LMS workshop at Derby undertook dozens of J39 repairs on behalf of the Eastern Region. Twice No.64784 visited Derby, in 1950 and in 1952. After that the workshop visits settled down and Stratford undertook all the remaining overhauls concerning this engine. When condemnation took place the 0-6-0 was sent to Doncaster for cutting up which seemed, at the time, to be a waste of resource as most of the other Stratford maintained J39's were being dealt with by Stratford during that period. Perhaps Doncaster had spare capacity and Stratford was chockerblock with condemned engines?. *BLP - DB780.*

One type of locomotive which will be forever associated with Stratford will be the 0-6-0 tank engines of LNER classes J67, J68 and J69. This is J69/2 No.68513 which started life as a J67 in November 1890 and was still going strong on the August day in 1959 when Don Beecroft photographed it on the shed yard at Stratford with more than a year of operational life still in it. The six-coupled tank engine had been built at Stratford works as GER No.401, a number which it kept until 7000 was added in 1924. At that time it was allocated to Peterborough East shed and only came to Stratford for works visits. In July 1935 it arrived at the works for a 'General' and after completion it stayed in London until November 1939 when Cambridge shed required its services, coincidentally immediately after a 'General' so it was good for another three years or so. Less than six months later it was transferred back to Stratford just in time for the most horrendous bombing campaign ever to engulf the British Isles. On 28th November 1942 it was sent to Parkeston but when the New Year arrived the 0-6-0T departed back to London where it was to stay until withdrawn on 18th October 1960. It received its second LNER number in October 1946 and its full BR number was applied during a 'General' at Stratford in May 1949. Of the one hundred and eighty 0-6-0T built under the banner of classes J67-69, most were built for working passenger trains on the intensive suburban services into and out of Liverpool Street station but fifty of them were constructed for shunting duties throughout the Great Eastern system and were therefore not equipped with the necessary braking equipment used in association with passenger stock. No.68513 was one of the latter type hence its residence at Peterborough by Grouping, well away from the hub bub of East London. In May/June 1952 this engine was rebuilt Class J69 Part 2 which indicated that it had a different boiler diagram than that previously carried. A fuller and much more detailed history of these GER 0-6-0 tank engines will appear in a future volume of Yeadon's Register to be published in early 2008. Note the 0-6-0 in the background has the correct version of the BR crest on its tender. *BLP - DB2955.*

Alongside the so-called 'New' shed on Sunday 15th June 1958 was this ex-works N7 No.69654 from Hatfield shed. The 0-6-2T had just completed a 'General' (its last) and has been nicely lined out. The unidentified N7 immediately behind contrasts well in the early afternoon sunshine, the J20 beyond is another which is in serious need of a clean. One of the contractor built members of the class, No.69654 was built during the LNER era when no less than one hundred and twenty-two N7's were constructed at various LNER workshops and by private locomotive builders. The N7 was another former GER design synonymous with Stratford and most of the class were allocated to the depot at one time or another. Even though No.69654 was stationed on the GN main line at the time of this photograph, it eventually migrated to Stratford to end its days although it did put in nearly twelve months work at 30A during 1960 before being condemned and eventually cut up at the adjacent locomotive works. *BLP - DB783.*

Stood over the ash pits outside Stratford engine shed, B17 No.61611 RAYNHAM HALL from Ipswich enjoys a Sunday break prior to working back home in June 1958. The Gresley B17 never did quite live up to what was expected of them but for twenty odd years before the coming of the BR 'Britannia' Pacifics they were the best available express passenger engines on offer to the former Great Eastern lines. This engine spent all of its twenty-nine year life working from the exGER sheds at Cambridge, Colchester, Ipswich, Norwich, Parkeston (only for one week in June 1946), and Stratford. However, for most of that time period it had to go out of the area for routine overhauls and heavy maintenance with Darlington, Doncaster and Gorton all having taken care of it whilst Stratford got a look-in sometimes although during the whole of the BR era it did not go near Stratford works once. Right at the end Doncaster's pull became too great and the 4-6-0 entered Doncaster 'Plant' on Wednesday 14th October 1959 and never came out, at least in one piece. The works responsible for its care during the last seven years of its life had finally condemned and scrapped this B17. *BLP - DB787.*

From which ever angle you viewed a Britannia Pacific they were impressive, very impressive. So too thought the GE Lines authority of BR when these locomotives became available to them from new in 1951. This is No.70030 WILLIAM WORDSWORTH on Stratford engine shed in August 1959. Not looking its best externally, it nevertheless appears to be able to 'do the business' and was indeed doing so. By now, of course, the GE Lines had got their English Electric Type 4 2,000 horsepower diesel electric locomotives which had taken over many of the East Anglia expresses from the 'Brits' but the big 7P engines were still at the forefront for the time being. No.70030 was a Norwich engine, one of the twenty-two 'Brits' allocated to Thorpe shed at this time. Initially Stratford shed had thirteen of these engines with the others allocated at Norwich but as the diesel-electric's became available Stratford took on the maintenance and well-being of the English Electric machines and the Pacifics gathered at 32A. A couple of the Britannia's had been allocated to Ipswich and Yarmouth for short periods after the arrival of the big diesels but by early 1959 Norwich became home for all the GE Lines Pacifics. *BLP - DB2635.*   35

Scenes such as this were commonplace at Stratford during the days of steam traction. Stratford built N7 No.69604 had spent the whole of its life allocated to 30A. Gorton built No.69633 had done likewise whilst contractor built No.69655, on the left, got to Stratford in January 1929 after spending just over three years at King's Cross (Top shed). It is now, however, early August 1959 and the winds of change are gathering momentum so although these three 0-6-2 tank engines appear to be resting during this sunny Sunday of the 9th day of the month, they are in fact waiting for the decision which would send them all to the scrap yard. The decision came on the Monday morning and all three were condemned together. Note that the BR crest on 69604's tank is one of the wrong versions which would not now be corrected. These N7's were cut up at Stratford shortly afterwards. *BLP - DB2637.*

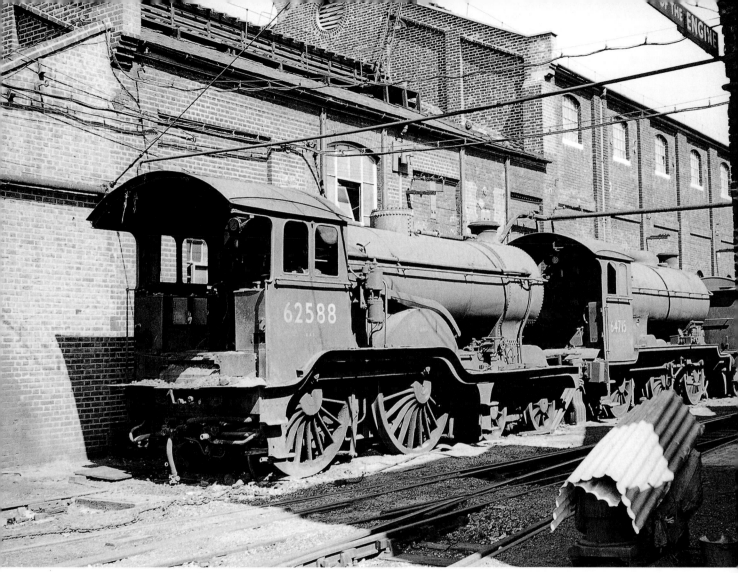

D16 Part 3 No.62588 had been withdrawn from service at Stratford Works in October 1958 but with its boiler was still useable the engine was then employed until June 1959 as a temporary steam supply for the workshops. It never got Stationary Boiler status and remained fairly intact, except for the missing dome cover, and even kept its coupling rods. By 9th August 1959, when this scene was captured, the engine was awaiting cutting up along with dozens of others stored around Stratford at that time. The 4-4-0 had been a Cambridge engine at withdrawal and had been allocated to various 'Country' sheds since 1947, the last time it had been allocated to Stratford. Besides working in its native patch around the GE lines, this engine had undertaken two forays away during its lifetime. In September 1934 it was transferred to Botanic Gardens shed in Hull for a month. Then, in April 1950, it went to Trafford Park shed and ended up working on the Cheshire Lines system for more than two years. It even managed a 'Casual' overhaul at Doncaster during that time. In front is J39 No.64715, a stranger to this part of the world which ventured south to Stratford Works from Colwick in March 1959 only to be condemned in May after pointlessly waiting around for a decision as to its future. The inevitable occurred and this unhappy pair are now waiting yet again for the short haul to the cutting-up shop. *BLP - DB2640.*

Resident Stratford J20 No.64685 rests outside the 'New' shed on Sunday 9th August 1959. This 0-6-0 was recently out of works after a 'Casual Light' repair in June. It was to visit the shops once more at the end of August and spend over a month having something put right under the same classified repair heading. Whatever was wrong must have been put right because the J20 did not visit works again before withdrawal in October 1960. The WD 'Austerity' behind the 0-6-0 appears to be in better external condition and the N7 on the left is positively sparkling. Stratford's famous and unique mechanical coaling plant dominates the background, its huge open air bunkers holding all grades of coal which in 1959 varied in quality from rubbish to reasonable. Note the door of the shed is still intact at this late date - unusual to say the least. *BLP-DB2642.*

J15 No.65476 stands alongside the 'New' shed at Stratford in August 1959. The 0-6-0 had not been near the works since a 'General' in October 1956 but it managed to stay operational until September 1962 when it was condemned on the 5th of that month, preceding the mass cull of former GER locomotives which occurred eleven days later. Unusually for engines from this class, it was purchased for scrap by a private dealer and was cut up at a yard in Great Bridge before the end of the year. This engine shed was opened in 1871 and although new at the time it was certainly superseded in the youthful stakes by the 'Jubilee' shed opened some sixteen years later in 1887. However, the name seems to have stuck because the site chosen for the shed was on new ground away from the locomotive facilities of the day which were centred around the old works. The 'new' shed, on 'new' ground heralded the way for the ongoing expansion of the Stratford site. The shed had been re-roofed in the meantime and it managed to outlive the 'Jubilee' shed by a number of years. One of its latter uses was to store locomotives from the National Collection. *BLP - DB2643.*

B2 No.61644 EARLHAM HALL was the last on Gresley's B17 class to be rebuilt to a two-cylinder engine and it was the only one done by British Railways. All ten of the class were allocated to sheds within the boundaries of the former Great Eastern Railway and all were maintained at Stratford Works. By the end of 1956 the B2's were all working from Cambridge shed but less than two years later withdrawals had started. In this August 1959 picture No.61644 is stabled on the yard at the west end of the 'Jubilee' shed at Stratford along with a resident J39 and J17 No.65555. No less than four different types of tender served the B2 class; one had a Group Standard 4200 gallon type; two were coupled to the tenders left behind by the Gresley 2-8-2 coal engines when they were scrapped; four had tenders from scrapped NER Atlantics which had coal rails running the full length of the tender and were curved at both end; finally, the last three also had tenders from withdrawn NE Atlantics but these tenders had much shorter coal rails which stopped a the rear of the bunker. No.61644 had one of the latter variety which were very distinctive with the squared off coal rails (plated over by now). The 4-6-0 appears to be in fairly good condition outwardly but it is nearly two years since it was last given a 'General' and its boiler needed renewal. Inevitably the end came in November when it was the penultimate member of the class. The last one No.61607 quickly followed in the middle of December. Once again, Stratford had complete control of the class and all of the B2's were cut up there. *BLP - DB2662.*

The B17's didn't have it any easier in 1959 but this one, No.61608 GUNTON managed to outlive the more modern B2 by about four months. It too was a Cambridge based engine but was under Doncaster works for maintenance and overhauls as were the rest of the B17's by now. The 4-6-0 is hiding its front end, where the Westinghouse pump is still fitted, just inside the west end of the 'Jubilee' shed. Up to a few months previously, this shed was some twelve roads wide as originally built in 1887 but in August 1959, as can be seen, it was down to being just six roads wide. The part of the shed covering the six northerly tracks had recently been demolished to make way for two, back to back, purpose built, four road diesel depots which were to become the heart of the GE Lines diesel maintenance empire. A new diesel multiple unit serving shed had already been built on the site of some former coal stacking ground between the 'Jubilee' and High Meads and that was in use by early 1959. This remaining portion of the 'Jubilee' shed would disappear once steam was eliminated from Stratford. Rebuilding of this shed had taken place in 1949 using concrete and brick but it had been rebuilt to house steam locomotives and was not in the modern, glass clad, airy style of the new era so, it had to go. Such was the pace of the BR Modernisation programme that ten years was too wide a gap to bridge with the existing infrastructure. Instead, money had to be spent if modernisation was to be given a chance. For the record, B17 No.61608 was cut up at Stratford rather than Doncaster. *BLP - DB2646.*

Thompson L1 No.67704 with another of its kind alongside, is bathing in the midday sun at the north end of the 'Jubilee' shed at Stratford on Sunday 9th August 1959. Outwardly the neglect was fairly obvious during this period but inward neglect had not really taken place as the fitters, boilersmiths and their small army of assistants battled to keep the steam locomotive fleet going. However, a losing battle was being fought on the front line of the shed fitting shop because the generals were no longer supporting their troops and in most cases had deserted them. It was an interesting period in railway history especially for those who were there. As for those who were not, well they probably find it all pretty hard to swallow as some of the facts seem more like inflated claims, figures appear exaggerated, the waste unforgivable. Like I said - interesting times. The whole of the L1 class migrated to Darlington whenever overhaul or maintenance was required and No.67704 would make that long trek during the coming December for new cylinders to be fitted (Casual Heavy). At the beginning of February 1960 it was back at Stratford but then, in November, it was condemned, aged twelve. Shortly afterwards it was hauled back to Darlington for cutting up. Note yet another incorrect BR crest. *BLP - DB2649.*

Forward in time now to March 1960 and Peppercorn K1 No.62015 takes on water from one of the columns at the east end of the 'Jubilee' shed yard. Looking very shabby, the ten year old 2-6-0 was one of five K1's on the Stratford strength at this time. In the left background can be seen evidence of the new motive power at 30A with one of the 1958-built North British Loco. Co. Type 1 Bo-Bo diesels standing on one of the roads of the soon to open diesel servicing and maintenance depot. Note the rather smart 16-ton mineral wagon which was being used to bring equipment for the new facility: nothing was too good for the diesels. No.62015 left Stratford about eighteen months after this scene was captured on film. It was luckier than most of the other Stratford steam locomotives and transferred to Retford via a fortnight at March depot. The K1 ended its days at Frodingham at the end of July 1965 and was sold for scrap to a famous (infamous?) scrapyard in Hull where on 8th November 1965 it was broken up. *BLP - DB2942.*

With some Sunday overtime being available, or was it simply his shift?, a young fitter enjoys a break in the late morning sunshine outside the lifting shop at Stratford engine shed in August 1959. The lifting shop was situated at the western end of the 'New' shed yard, alongside the coaling plant. The actual lifting was done outside the building by what can only be described as modern steel framed sheerlegs. Inside the building there was no such appliance for lifting anything large so all the lifting was done outside. Once the wheel set of the affected locomotive, or tender, was taken out, the engine or wheels would be taken into the shop' and dealt with accordingly. J19 No.64663 appears dumped but its future is still secure - for the time being anyway. The line on which the 0-6-0 stands was a through road, rather than a siding, linking the shed throat to the turntable at the western end of the yard so perhaps a bit of shunting was going on here - Don Beecroft's notes do not elucidate on the activity. *BLP - DB2645.*

Cambridge based Thompson B2 No.61607 BLICKLING was to become the last of the class when No.61644 was condemned in November 1959 but only for three weeks because it's time came on Monday 14th December. The original Gresley design, the B17, was to outlive the Thompson rebuild by eight months but the circumstances of the B2's operational area had more to do with their earlier demise rather than any design flaw. In June 1958, fresh from a 'General' at Stratford (the last given to any of the class), the 4-6-0 is seen under Primrose Street bridge outside Liverpool Street station waiting to use the turntable prior to working back home. This former B17 was rebuilt to B2 standard at Darlington in May 1947 and came out from that with a new Diagram 100A boiler. In order to determine the advantages of the B2 over the B17, a number of tests were conducted in late 1945 between newly converted B2 No.2871 MANCHESTER CITY and B17/1 No.2827 ASKE HALL. The trials saw the engines working the same trains on alternate days and the concluding evidence put the B2 on top. More exhaustive tests with a dynamometer car were carried out in October 1947 using this engine and B17/6 No.1622 ALNWICK CASTLE, which also had a 100A boiler fitted. The B17 now came out on top in all respects and was deemed superior to the B2. So, the boiler was a good one but the rebuilt engines were not in the end necessary and simply reboilering the B17 would have done the job with a better result. One point for Thompson and one against. *BLP - DB769.*

B17/6 No.61666 NOTTINGHAM FOREST stands at the buffer stops on platform 6 at Liverpool Street station in August 1959. The train which it brought into the terminus was from Yarmouth and with fresh motive power at its head it is about to depart for the coast. In August 1959 this B17 was allocated to Colchester engine shed and had been since April 1954. The 4-6-0 had worked on GE metals since July 1944 after spending seven years working on the former Great Central route between Manchester (London Road) and London (Marylebone). During that period it was variously allocated to Woodford Halse, Neasden and finally Gorton from 22nd August 1939 to 23rd July 1944. Both Doncaster and Gorton workshops took care of its maintenance needs for the most part but Stratford carried out the occasional major overhaul including the rebuilding to Part 6. Stratford also scrapped the engine after it was condemned in March 1960. *BLP - DB2702.*

We saw Britannia No.70030 WILLIAM WORDSWORTH earlier on in this album at Stratford shed and here is how the Pacific got to London on that day - on an express from Norwich. There are no carriages now, the train has returned north with another 'Brit' in charge, or was it an EE Type 4? - no matter. Here at Liverpool Street station in August 1959 the unkempt 4-6-2 is seen reversing out of the terminus en route to Stratford shed for servicing and a layover until its next working. The lofty roof of the train shed at the London terminus is well depicted here as is the proximity of Broad Street station at its higher elevation on the right. *BLP - DB2703.*

Another filthy Norwich 'Britannia' No.70002 GEOFFREY CHAUCER, with its number just visible, slowly backs onto its train at Liverpool Street in August 1959. The horizon is dominated by the viaduct of Broad Street station approaches but that terminus ended up being but a shadow of the Liverpool Street complex. In the early 1860's the Eastern Counties Railway, precursor of the Great Eastern asked the North London Railway if they could use their new London terminus when it was completed but the NLR refused the ECR and so Liverpool Street station was born. The ECR and Great Eastern never looked back whereas the parochial North London outfit never quite made the big time, even with L&NWR backing. Over on the West Side an L1, No.67702 and an unidentified N7 fuss around coaching stock prior to the introduction of electrification on that side of the station. *BLP - DB2704.*

Keeping up the, by now, daily 'tradition' of supplying grime encrusted 'Britannia's' for its premier expresses, the Great Eastern area appeared to be trying to run before it could walk with the new diesel motive power at its disposal. The day of the 'Brits' on the London-Norwich services was nearly at an end although diesel failures during the period up to the end of 1961 kept them firmly on the reserve bench with occasional first team action. With its corporate identity masked, No.70012 JOHN OF GAUNT stands waiting for the signal to hurry away with a Norwich service on Saturday 15th August 1959. BR was spending vast amounts of money on the suburban and country services running out of Liverpool Street, the one time direct current electric multiple units were being changed to alternating current and all the relevant wiring was being upgraded. The Shenfield stock was being converted at Stratford Carriage & Wagon works whilst new stock was coming from places such as Wolverton and York. Literally hundreds of new carriages were to be introduced over the next few years. The Liverpool Street-Clacton and Walton services would require over 250 vehicles by the end of 1963, all to be constructed at York. Track was being lowered to accommodate the new 25kV. catenary, bridges were being heightened for clearance. The transformation was going to be massive. However, locomotive hauled trains would continue to rule the long distance services to Norwich and beyond and diesels would be the prime motive power for a number of decades before electrification reached those isolated enclaves. In the meantime steam was having its last moments of glory before being exiled to places far beyond the Eastern Region. A nine and a half hour daytime survey carried out by a number of enthusiasts at Liverpool Street during the Saturday in question revealed that 145 main line departures and arrivals were headed by 36 Thompson B1's, 13 Britannia's, 10 B17's, 5 Peppercorn K1's and 5 Gresley K3's. For the record 15 Type 2 diesel locomotives were also involved with main line trains but none of the EE Type 4's were logged. Two days previously a B12, No.61535 had charge of an evening service to Cambridge. *BLP - DB2705.*

N7 No.69614 was specially painted and burnished in 1956 to carry out the duties of the Liverpool Street station West Side pilot. In March 1960, looking very much the part and in total contrast to the majority of the steam locomotives still using the terminus, the 0-6-2 tank whistles intent to proceed to another area of the station where its services were required. Note that it wears the incorrect version of the BR crest but it was due to go into Stratford Works for a Casual Heavy overhaul about a month after this scene was recorded so a new 'correct' version of the crest was probably applied then. Built at Stratford and coming into traffic one the first day of the first month of 1924, the N7 was Stratford based for most of its life with a couple of short interludes on the old GN and the GC during its first few years of working. Parkeston shed also had it for a couple of years in the early part of the BR period but other than that it can claim to be a Stratford lad. It certainly ended its days there after being abruptly condemned in December 1960. J69 No.68619 was another regular 'pilot' at Liverpool Street and had been on that duty since 1948. In July 1956 the 0-6-0T had its coupling rods painted red to keep up the tradition of distinction for the job - the N7 quickly followed and had its coupling rods painted. Apparently an official instruction was issued that both engines were to be cleaned on a daily basis and it appears that the N7 is having the benefit of that daily spit and polish. Lurking behind No.69614 is an unidentified Brush Type 2, one of a class which was to make a big impact on the former Great Eastern lines over the following decade. *BLP - DB2952.*

When the Eastern Region of British Railways took over the London, Tilbury & Southend line they also inherited its motive power and rolling stock, although the former would still visit Derby Works on the London Midland Region for overhauls. One particular former LMS class of locomotive was the Stanier 3-cylinder 4P 2-6-4 tank engines, numbered 42500 to 42536, which were introduced in 1934 purely for working the LT&SR passenger services. One of those, No.42515 is seen in July 1957 heading a Fenchurch Street to Southend express through Pitsea station. These engines were amongst the heaviest of the LMS Standard tank engines and weighing in at over 92 tons they were nearly five tons heavier than their 2-cylinder cousins. By July 1957 all thirty-seven of the class were allocated to Shoeburyness shed. At the London end of the Southend line, Plaistow shed used to house some of them at various periods; for instance on the last day of the LMS Shoeburyness depot had the first twenty-two allocated numerically with Plaistow having Nos.2522 to 2536. Besides these Stanier tanks Plaistow, at that time, also had thirteen of the 2-cylinder Fairburn 2-6-4T, introduced in 1945, to balance the numbers. By 1957, however, Plaistow had gained sixteen of the newer BR Standard 2-6-4 Class 4 tanks to supplement their Fairburn stud and keep the status quo with Shoeburyness. Pitsea was the junction of the direct line from Fenchurch Street via Upminster to Southend, and the Tilbury line which basically followed the course of the Thames. Note the length of the train made up of eight non-corridor suburban carriages - standard for the line. *BLP - DB444.*

At Tilbury a triangle of lines was formed which enabled through trains to stop at Tilbury (Town) station before the routes diverged to either the terminus at Tilbury (Riverside) or proceed via the north side of the triangle to Pitsea. Within the triangle an engine shed, accessible from the southern tip of the triangle adjacent to Riverside station, was built as early as 1854 but this two road building was superseded in 1912 by a four road shed erected by the Midland Railway who now operated the line. That particular shed was rebuilt in 1956 but the LMS had spent money in the meantime on a small mechanical coaling plant. Also within the triangle of lines was a hamlet of thirty-two railway cottages, each with a garden and formed in three separate rows. In July 1957 another of the LMS built 3P 4-4-2 tank engines, No.41978, is either reversing down to Riverside station or is heading for the shed from the station. The eastern leg of the triangle can be seen just below the horizon. It meets with this the western leg just prior to the road bridge in the right background. Tilbury July 1957. It was here at Tilbury that Henry VIII built a fort to watch over the Thames and where, in 1588, Elizabeth I addressed the army she had gathered and swore to take up arms with them to repel a Spanish invasion which may have occurred if the Armada had not been defeated by the Navy. Steam was defeated on this line in 1962 when full electrification took place and all the steam locomotives were either scrapped or sent to pastures anew. Tilbury engine shed closed on 18th June 1962 - surplus to requirements. *BLP - DB442.*

Southend-on-Sea (Central) station was not the terminus of the LT&SR line, that was through more stations further east at Shoeburyness. In July 1957 the station pilot duties were being performed by this LMS 1930 Derby built 4-4-2T, No.41977. By now the Atlantic tanks were past their prime and many of the LMS built engines had either been scrapped or were getting near to that event. This particular 3P design had first seen the light of day in 1897, although those early Thomas Whitelegg engines had been rebuilt during the period 1905 to 1911 and formed the basis for what became known as the 'Tilbury Tanks'. No.41977 was allocated to Plaistow shed at this time, its unkempt appearance reinforcing that fact. However, the 4-4-2T carried on working on the line until withdrawn in February 1959, along with all the others of its class still operational. Some classmates had left the LT&SR shortly after BR came into being and ended up at diverse locations such as Skipton, Toton, Stratford, Colchester and even Peterborough. One of those, No.41969 lasted until March 1960, appropriately at March shed but whether it performed any work there is unknown. *BLP - DB425.*

Cambridge based Thompson B2 No.61607 BLICKLING was apparently employed on station pilot duties at Ipswich when Don Beechroft photographed it in July 1957. The 4-6-0 appears busy as it draws down to couple up to a pair of vehicles dropped off by a previous working - wonder where from? *BLP - DB427.*

So, we have out first immaculately turned out 'Britannia'. Thorpe based No.70007 COEUR-de-LION has charge of an Up Norwich express and is blowing off at the Ipswich stop in July 1957. The 'Brits' were well liked by the GE men and as long as the tubes were kept clean an clear these engines could easily handle their trains with ease. The 7MT's were diagrammed intensively and if any Region got their money's worth from these machines it was the GE. Of course, as mentioned earlier, until 1951 the 4-6-0 of B1, B12 and B17 classes were the best that Norwich and Stratford could muster so these Pacifics were very welcome additions to the fleet. By the summer of 1961 the Britannia's had had their day on the premier expresses of the GE lines, the diesels had at last taken over. After ten years the big engines were relegated, ironically, to mixed traffic duties and were in the main sent to March shed. Admitted, that place was still in the Region but its duties did not include haulage of the crack expresses. 'The Lionheart' was the last 'Brit' to leave Norwich depot, transferring to March shed in November 1961. From there it went to Carlisle Kingmoor in December 1963. Whilst it was attending Crewe Works for overhaul in June 1965 it was condemned and cut up - the first of the class to go. *BLP - DB431.*

Local B12 No.61564 waiting in the middle road at Ipswich station to take over an Up express in July 1957. This engine had undergone a 'General' during the winter of 1956-57 and would attend Stratford once more during the year for a 'Casual Light' 16th September to 3rd October. After that it would carry on for another full year before becoming a casualty in the GE Line quest to rid steam from the area as soon as possible. Note the young train spotter on platform 3 with his ABC. Wonderful days indeed. *BLP - DB434.*

Slowing for the Ipswich stop, 'Britannia' No.70012 JOHN OF GAUNT coasts into the station with a Down Norwich express in July 1957. Our previous illustration of this engine in 1959 at Liverpool Street station (page 49) revealed a much neglected livery compared with this showing. Of course, at this time it was a Norwich engine and had been since new in May 1951. The train is made up of a mixture of Gresley, Thompson and BR vehicles - something of a hybrid really and a bit like the GE Line in the 50's. *BLP - DB448.*

For our last look at Ipswich station we find another 4-6-0 on station pilot work in mid July 1957. B17/6 No.61649 SHEFFIELD UNITED was in the carriage sidings shortly after coming home to 32B from a 'General' at Doncaster. This 'Footballer' had been allocated to Ipswich since July 1946, during that time it had spent nearly three weeks at Yarmouth South Town in October 1949. Its introduction to GE Lines was rather late compared with most of its class because initially it went new from Darlington Works to Doncaster shed on 9th March 1936. On 26th of that month it transferred to the GC route and was sent to Leicester Central shed. At the end of May 1940 it returned to the GN main line but allocated to New England depot until 29h July when it moved to Norwich and a near six year residence there. Like other B17's, this engine was passed around from workshop to workshop with no one establishment seemingly responsible for their upkeep. Darlington, Doncaster, Gorton and Stratford all had a hand in their maintenance over the years. Even when they were resident on the GE lines in BR days most of the class passed through Gorton shops two or three times before Doncaster eventually took them on from the mid-50's. *BLP - DB435.*

The terminal station at Maldon East & Heybridge, to give it its full name (population 6,590 in 1927 and 43 miles from Liverpool Street), stood at the eastern end of the branch from Witham on the main line. The latter station is still with us but Maldon East closed in 1964 being no part of the electrification plans on the GE line This is Maldon East station in July 1957 being spruced up and receiving some serious maintenance to its ornate buildings. A station was established here in 1848 by the Eastern Counties Railway no doubt with visions of grandeur judging from the style of buildings erected, although only one platform was provided and that remained the case until closure of the station in 1964. Besides the station there was also a two-road brick built engine shed built at the same time and this housed the engines working the trains to Witham and those taking trains along the branch via Maldon West to Woodham Ferrers and Wickford. At the latter two named places there were turntables and servicing areas for the Maldon engines. The engine shed at Maldon East (immediately behind the photographer) closed in November 1959, a victim of dieselisation on the branch. However, in July 1957 everything was running to normal as it had over the previous 110 years and the branch train from Witham (there were two intermediate stations, Wickham Bishops and Langford & Ulting) had just arrived. Stratford based F5 No.67195 had charge of the four-coach train which was made up from some ancient looking rolling stock. Maldon West station, along with Cold Norton and the two Halts on the branch to Woodham Ferres closed in 1939. Uncoupling from its train, No.67195 would make its way to the turntable off picture, to the left of the station, turn, top up its side tanks from the windpump assisted water source, run round its train and couple onto the other end ready for its next journey to Witham. Idyllic existence? How times have changed. The F5 did not live long enough to be evicted from the branch by the diesels because in May 1958 it was condemned and cut up at Stratford. No doubt there was still plenty of other tank engines available for this job. In the early summer of 1958 J15's were employed on the passenger turns hauling just two coaches. The German diesel railbuses (E79961-79964) were waiting in the wings and on 7th July 1958 one of them took over the passenger service on the branch. The planner's had originally pencilled-in that the railbus was to run the service in the quiet periods during the daytime with, however, it was found that the railbus could not meet the demand upon its meagre proportions and a two-car Craven's unit had to be employed for the 1958 summer traffic between Witham and Maldon - J15's and a couple of carriages filled-in between the diesel blips. A 'first day story' worth repeating is the one about the Maldon driver who, on the premier occasion of the railbus services, wore his best suit only to have the railbus fail on him during the morning. He finished his shift driving a J15! *BLP - DB436.*

Besides an engine being employed for the Maldon branch passenger duties, there was also another tank for shunting the goods yards at both Maldon stations and the facilities at Wickham Bishops. In July 1957 one of the shunting versions of Class J68, No.68648, another Stratford based tank engine, exiled temporarily to Maldon East shed, gets a train ready for Witham in the goods yard at Maldon East. The yard at East station offered the full facilities to agents including a one and a half ton capacity crane. Livestock transit and other agricultural elements became good business for the railway here. Even in 1957 we can see farm machinery loaded on the flat wagon. Latterly Maldon has become famous for its sea salt production although this industry has always been just one of the town's maritime related occupations; boat building, fishing and coastal trading are three more. There is a 13th Century church in the town which has the only triangular tower in Britain. The population has now surpassed 15,000 but there is no railway station nor railway connection of any kind. Not wishing to show any bias towards this Great Eastern branch line but from a modelling point of view this location is a superb example of a branch terminus. It had everything for the BR period modeller - an ornate station, two-road engine shed with turntable, water tank and wind pump, goods yard with cattle dock and crane, wood yard with private siding, F5 and J67, J68, J69 tank engines, J15 tender engines, diesel railbus, Cravens d.m.u., 350 h.p. diesel shunter, a defunct junction. If you really wanted to stretch a point would could create a small quayside with appropriate boats. Food for thought? *BLP - DB439.*

Don Beecroft's visit to East Anglia in July 1957 was something of a marathon trying to cram in as much of the contemporary railway scene as was possible before the great changes began to alter the region for ever. At Colchester he caught local B17/6 No.61651 DERBY COUNTY passing the darkened bulk of the three-road engine shed as it swings onto the Down main with a Liverpool Street-Clacton train. This 4-6-0 had been to Doncaster earlier in the year for a 'general' but you wouldn't know that by the state of its paintwork now. Colchester based since December 1953, it moved to Cambridge in February 1959 to join the rest of its brethren there but six months later, on another visit to Doncaster, it was condemned and promptly cut up. The engine shed here fared no better, closing on 2nd November 1959 when a new purpose built diesel depot opened nearby. At least the engine shed lineage was carried on at Colchester, for the time being anyway, to add to a long line (in age terms) of engine sheds dating back to March 1843. *BLP - DB440.*

Passing one of the Ivatt Class 2 tender engines allocated to this place (Nos.46464 and 46465 were here from July 1951 to October 1959 when they transferred to Parkeston), 'Britannia' No.70012 approaches Colchester station with a Walton-on-Naze-Liverpool Street train in July 1957. Our popular Pacific was certainly busy during the month and it is nice to see that the cleaners have also been using some elbow grease. This train is made up almost entirely of BR Mk.1 carriages. Under the GE Lines electrification plans, Clacton-on-Sea was to get its own dedicated units along with Walton-on-Naze and during 1962-63 more that 250 vehicles were built at York, including eight Griddle cars for those who ate a hearty 'full English' on the way to Town travelling at 90 m.p.h. Even the so-called 'Clacton units' are history now but in July 1957 they were some planner's 'pie in the sky'. *BLP - DB445.*

It wasn't until 1968 that Swaffam station closed completely but prior to that the branch to Thetford via Roudham Junction was closed in June 1964. In July 1957 the station was still fully operational and we see here a Norwich bound passenger train in the charge of J17 No.65533. This King's Lynn based 0-6-0 had been fitted with a vacuum ejector and steam heating in 1944 prior to it transferring to the M&GN line at South Lynn shed in June of that year. However, its time on the 'Joint' line was curtailed in September 1951 when the Ivatt Cl.4 2-6-0 tender engines started to take on the M&GN services. Cambridge was the recipient then but in February 1952 it was sent to the London, Tilbury & Southend line and was stationed at Plaistow. For operating on that line the engine had to be fitted was AWS which was fitted at Bow Works in March 1952. In May 1955, with the coming of the BR Standard Cl.4 tanks engines to the LT&SR, the 0-6-0 returned to familiar pastures and was allocated to Norwich but in September King's Lynn required its services and that where it ecked out a living for the rest of its life to withdrawal in January 1960. Swaffam, Norfolk, fifteen miles south-east of King's Lynn, had a small population of just over 2,900 in 1927 but that has virtually doubled today. One hundred and eleven miles from Liverpool Street, the town was founded by an Anglo-Saxon tribe - the Swaefas - who gave their name to the place. For many years it was concerned with the woollen trade. The goods yard here could boast a full measure of facilities and there were, up to nationalisation, no less that five private sidings serving local industry. *BLP - DB441.*

MARCH ENGINE SHED

For our last look at the Great Eastern lines during the British Railways era we travel to what might be termed the northern extremity of the old GER, not the farthest outposts such as the satellites at Lincoln and Doncaster but the northern border of the territory so to speak - March, Cambridgeshire. This great cross-roads of freight trains was to become one of the most important marshalling yards in the country with five separate routes converging on this one time quiet, boggy, windswept fenland. The first engine shed was erected in 1850 by the Eastern Counties Railway. In 1870 this was replaced by a three-road shed built by the GER. The first inkling of what was to become of this backwater occurred in 1884 when the sidings were laid at Whitemoor and a new six-road engine shed was built. The Joint line was opened through Spalding, Sleaford, Lincoln and Gainsborough to reach the coalfields which so eluded the Great Eastern. The yards started to grow and by Grouping further enlargements were required by the LNER. A new Up yard mirrored the old but now newly named Down yard with the Joint line bisecting them. A new engine shed of ten roads was established in 1932 but only five roads were covered leaving the outside five for 'turnaround' preparation. A large mechanical coaling plant of the 'Cenotaph' variety with 500 tons capacity had been erected in 1925 during previous alterations to the shed yard. March Whitemoor was now in business for its strategic role during the horrific conflict some seven years away. Having got through WWII relatively unscathed, considering its importance and its proximity to so many bomber bases, March settled in to the role of sorting the freight vital to the country's post-war recovery. Ten years later, under a new regime, the place was still very busy in June 1956. With its tender piled so high it is just within the loading gauge, B17/6 No.61619 WELBECK ABBEY employs extension boards in the coal space as it waits to enter the maintenance shed for a defect to be rectified. Within a few weeks it would be off to Doncaster for its last 'General' and repaint. In the right background goods engines crowd the yard of 'The Washout' shed.

BLP - DB114.

B2 No.61616 FALLODON stands in the engine yard alongside the six-road 1884 shed in June 1959. The line of 350 h.p. 0-6-0 diesel shunters is headed by D3494, note the small 'D' in place of the '1' prefix. Already this depot has a large complement of these shunting locomotives but other bigger diesels were to come as part of the East Anglian diesel scheme and for that occasion a new three-road diesel depot was being planned for and which was to be sited on the north side of this shed - right where the 1925 built four road shed stood - demolition was required. In the meantime, the old shed here was to be utilised to maintain the diesels, the 'Washout' shed would never do because it was both busy, smoky and dirty. The B2 would soon work home to Cambridge and within a couple of months would become scrap.
BLP - DB1982.

65

Also 'on shed' that day in June 1959 was J17 No.65583. The 0-6-0 was spending its third stint at the Cambridgeshire depot having come here firstly in May 1924 from Lincoln. It was to spend twenty-four years at March before going off to South Lynn and a nine month spell on the M&GN. On its return to March in September August 1949 it came straight from Stratford Works having had a 'General' and the title BRITISH RAILWAYS applied to its tender. In September 1953 Bury St Edmunds shed needed a J17 for four months and No.65583 was duly sent. On return from there the 0-6-0 put in another seven years work from March before moving finally to Norwich in September 1961, swapped for a 'Britannia' Pacific. Five months later No.65583 was condemned nearly forty-two years old. Note the wrongly facing crest on the tender which in the event was never corrected on this or any other J17. To the right is a Thompson O1, a class with long associations to March depot since their introduction during WWII. *BLP - DB1984.*

To add to the fog created by the stabled engines, the depot's sand drying furnace contributes more pollution to the Fenland air. This is March in April 1960 with the five roads of the 1932-built 'Washout' shed easily depicted by the longitudinal ventilators atop the northlight roof. We are in the area of the daily great gathering for engines arriving from far and wide - classes galore and all seemingly different. There might be a myriad of classes depicted here and on the following pages but they all have one thing in common - grime. Nearest our camera is J19/2 No.64646, a visitor from Cambridge which had spent much of its BR life working on the M&GN. At withdrawal, in October 1961, it kept up with the previous Great Northern connection in its life and was cut up at Doncaster. To the left is an unidentified Stanier 8F whilst behind the J19 is a Midland Region 4F 0-6-0 which is equally anonymous by dint of its number being obscured by filth. *BLP - DB3248.*

You can see why the Clean Air Act was introduced. We have now moved up the yard slightly towards the north end to view our next visitor. This is Stanier mogul No.42972 from Crewe South which has been turned, coaled and watered ready to work back home via Peterborough, Stamford, Leicester and Nuneaton - probably. The Coaling plant operator, or the March disposal gang, certainly knew how to fill a locomotive tender to capacity. Just look at those tenders - no shortage at this place then. Alongside No.42972 is J20 No.64684, another Cambridge engine on a day out but also on its last legs - it was condemned at the end of June in need of a new boiler. This was another former March engine which had transferred to Cambridge in November 1959. *BLP - DB3249.*

Keeping the old GER traditions alive, D16/3 No.62613 was a relative newcomer to March depot having transferred from Spital Bridge shed at the end of January 1960. It was not long for this world and was called to Stratford in October and dispatched shortly afterwards. Just beyond the 4-4-0 is K3 No.61861, a local lad which was to transfer to Colwick in January 1961. On the same road at the D16 is a very grimy WD - weren't they all? - which is also coaled and ready for off. The WD 'Austerity' 2-8-0 was another large goods engine which had associations with this depot since the class was introduced during WWII. Prior to their shipment to Europe after D-Day, many of these useful engines were stationed here. On their return from the Continent in the immediate post-war years, they once again re-acquainted themselves with March being allocated in their dozens and never left the place until steam was banished from the depot in December 1963. Behind the WD is another Stanier 2-8-0 - this was a freight depot. *BLP - DB3250.*

Ready to charge up the Joint line to Doncaster and then home to the North Eastern Region at York is B16 No.61478. This was one of the class which had to be renumbered in December 1949 so that its original number - 1409 - could be taken up by a new Thompson B1, with a '6' added. As far as the grime situation goes in this sequence of pictures, it is as though there was a competition being played out between the depots to operate the dirtiest locomotive. No wonder the image portrayed by BR at this time was a poor one. Certainly standards had gone beyond slipping away, it was more like driving away. Trainspotters had a rough old time when passing most sheds in a train, even at low speed you could not see most of the numbers of the engines on shed. At least the B16 number would have been discernible but only until December 1960 because Darlington Works called the 4-6-0 in and promptly condemned it. Also ready to work north along the 'Joint' is Doncaster based V2 No.60899 which is standing behind the B16 and is mainly obscured. The V2 was once resident at this place, for five years in fact, from May 1952 to June 1957 when it transferred to King's Cross. *BLP - DB3252.*

In amongst the throng at March depot in April 1960 was this Thompson O1 No.63590, snuggled up to a WD 2-8-0. Now, up until Grouping March shed had never had any eight-coupled locomotives to call its own but that all changed when the LNER came into being. The Robinson O4 was the First World War equivalent of the second conflict's WD 'Austerity' and the LNER, along with most other companies, purchased a fair number of them for a knock-down price. Most were allocated to sheds within the old GCR boundaries whilst some went to other Areas. March shed got its first O4's in 1924, two in fact but only for a few weeks. In 1925 three different 2-8-0s arrived then returned from whence they came within a few weeks but in 1929 no less than fourteen arrived and the relationship between March shed and Class O4 was cemented. Different one then came and went, staying for a couple of months or up to fifteen years in some cases. Altogether forty-eight different O4's have been allocated to March over the years since 1924. The last ones left in 1952 but by then the WD 'Austerity was entrenched at March. To supplement the O4 allocation a number of Gresley O2's were transferred to March shed in LNER days, fifteen of the 1930's built engines coming straight into traffic from Doncaster. Most of them had left in 1950, the growing band of WD's once again ousting out the old boys. This Thompson O1 was a visitor from Staveley, however, it was no stranger to March having been allocated to the place from 3rd March 1957 to 15th November 1959. It arrived at March depot in 1957 'mob handed' with twenty-four other O1's from Annesley shed. A number of them hung around to the end at March and at one point another O1 joined those in early 1963. It was in 1944 when two O1's joined the March allocation after being rebuilt from O4's but their initial residency was only until 1949. So, over the years the 2-8-0 type really made itself at home at March. For nearly forty years they had been the mainstay of the heavy mineral and goods train haulage to and from Whitemoor yard. *BLP - DB3254.*

With a 'Fire Brigade' C.E.D. wagon, No.DE940270, for company and K3 No.61845 looking on, J15 No.65458 stands out of the way at the southern end of the 'Washout' shed in April 1960. A recent addition to the March allocation, it is a reminder of what the Great Eastern Railway was all about for much of its existence - lightweight six-coupled goods engines and similar four-coupled passenger engines. The little 0-6-0 had seen many changes since it was put into traffic at Stratford in 1906. For the most part of its life it had been stationed right across the length and breadth of the old GE system from Southend to Stratford, from Colchester to Cambridge, from Norwich to March and even Parkeston. When new four-coupled engines had charge of the express passenger trains. Then came the 4-6-0 type, built so as not to enrage the Civil Engineer. Then came the Pacifics which revolutionised the schedules of the express passenger trains. Finally it saw the coming of the diesels and the rapid demise of the premier steam locomotives. On the day that this J15 was condemned the first 'Britannia' Pacifics were transferring to March Whitemoor shed - a freight depot first and foremost. Long after the J15 was cut up the diesels came and went from March, the sheds, old and new, were raised to the ground, the massive coaling plant having gone shortly after steam was exiled in 1963. The marshalling yards were silenced and this corner of Cambridgeshire returned to being open fenland once again. Some of the railway lines are still there as is the passenger station but there are no other markers of what else lay here once. *BLP - DB3262.*